the stones

the stones

by
dennis cooley

TURNSTONE PRESS

the stones

Turnstone Press
Artspace Building
206-100 Arthur Street
Winnipeg, MB
R3B 1H3 Canada
www.TurnstonePress.com

MIX
Paper from responsible sources
FSC® C016245

Turnstone Press gratefully acknowledges the assistance of the Canada Council for the Arts, the Manitoba Arts Council, the Government of Canada through the Canada Book Fund, and the Province of Manitoba through the Book Publishing Tax Credit and the Book Publisher Marketing Assistance Program.

Cover image: Morekai Rocks, New Zealand. Cover image provided by Wayne Watt.

Some of these poems appeared in earlier versions in *passwords*. An earlier version of "cenotaph" appeared in *correction line* and is included here with permission from Thistledown Press. "benchmark" will appear in a special issue of *Prairie Fire* in the fall of 2013 to celebrate the life and work of Birk Sproxton.

Printed and bound in Canada by Friesens for Turnstone Press.

Library and Archives Canada Cataloguing in Publication

Cooley, Dennis, 1944-, author
The stones / Dennis Cooley.

Poems.
ISBN 978-0-88801-449-8 (pbk.)

I. Title.

PS8555.O575S76 2013 C811'.54 C2013-905182-1

dedication:
for Diane who saw
almost all of the stones

And art exists that one may recover the sensation of life;
it exists to make one feel things, to make the stone stony. . .
—Victor Shklovsky

Till a' the seas gang dry, my dear,
And the rocks melt wi' the sun.
—Robert Burns

Inside the cathedral Diane and Bob butt their heads against the figure of a man who, legend has it, enjoyed exceptional wisdom. Tête-à-tête. Thus might they gain some of his genius.

At breakfast Kroetsch mentions once more the immense understanding he and Diane have acquired by knocking their heads against the statue. Not once did he hesitate. You two, he says (by which I take him to mean Dawne and I), are way behind, you failed to bang your heads against the stone, stupidly. And he laughs. I felt like a horse that'd been hammered, he says, I staggered back, stunned.

(Stoned, perhaps.)

—Santiago de Compostela, May 11–12, 2002

Sweet are the uses of adversity,
Which, like the toad, ugly and venomous,
Wears yet a precious jewel in his head.
And this our life, exempt from public haunt,
Finds tongues in trees, books in the running brooks,
Sermons in stones, and good in everything.
—William Shakespeare

the stones

Scotland is they say
\\a hard place
where sounds store in stones
and stories score on rock

a cryptic story
the dead slammed
open & shut

abandoned quarries the graveyards
littered with stone
jammed with bones
their own quarrels with the neighbours

& what if old pooch sniffing you stept
on them would they where they slept
granite with indignation cry out
hadn't we heard didn't we know

where they were

their memories
filed against time the stones
flaking in rain

stones everywhere
off-kilter
minerals rotting in water

stone a well time drips onto
pools worn away

everywhere stones stand or fall to their knees
into dampness scaling
up and down Princess Street forever aware of itself
under Scott's unblinking across

the street before the trains he has turned
his back on rains
sift the scooped-out valley and golfers
quickened by a small gust of light thwack
giant hail stones

as fate would have it or human hand
broken by lightning in 1922
the pierced rock, not granite

nor amper
sand though it is sand
stone settled
on the bottom of the sea stands
on the edge of the world

in the souris valley
which is to say SIR-iss
the world pulverizing in service to

a blow-torch sun whooshes
into crevices curls
inside crack & fissure
the rocks scraped by wind and snow
and by later arrivals
rivals for space
who flanked animals
on the stones pigment
dug the alphabet of their names into
the pebbled skin and what is left
falls off in flakes & sometimes shelves

the challenge
to find under
the leavings
traces of paint shadow lines
left by the Stone Sioux
called Assiniboine
buffalo elk bison thunder
bird and teepee wind

carried away in our hands
faint residue of picto
graphs photo

graphs snap
shots in which we
remove and
can almost

see
sketchy
outlines on
the paper

cenotaph
fr kenos empty + taphon tomb

i
an empty tomb
cynosure to an emptied town
who then risen
rinsed in weak november
sun the head stone there the names
then that were recalled
two sets & more the men

buried there not there but there
when they called
were called

their names a skim of snow
& feet in rubber
boots air chill & thin as kerosene

school kid on remembrance day
all of them red with poppies pinned
stamping cold from foot to foot &
the South Saskatchewan Regiment
loved and were loved & now
time flaps in our coats
& time waited in the tomb
beside it ten years earlier
when there was only one list

HILL 70 ARRAS PASSCHENDAELE
AMIENS CAMBRAI MONS YPRES
ST. ELOI SOMME COURCELETTE
VIMY RIDGE HILL 80

the letters
in black stains leak
mascara from women's faces weeping

ii

they must have shone there the Mounties
THE RCMP
bright as coral as blood
stones all those corporals
they must have looked like poppies
in bright tunics & yellow stripes
they stemmed themselves on
when they dammed the red tide
in aura almost incorporeal

spelt capitals in september air
before the coal
miners died inside

long lines the rifles wrote
comic book balloons **BANG BANG**
cowboys & indians all over again

pinned red flowers to them
the men with unspellable names
        almost unsayable names
in early fall turning into corpses
in acts of elision & rewriting

the tuniced men stuttered
      in acronyms at the corners
  when they read & answered
the antonyms & anonyms the miners
written in when the police resolved
to forward them to the coroner

                                        the ink spilled in dust
                                        the strange men knelt
                                        & dug & died in
spelled the darkness they wore & worked

they were tangled letters their names
fell into The Mercury **splat** they split badly
                mangled &   startled
      started into history

before (and after) other uniforms & other names
                not gray /red
their own versions of mayhem
maimed mauled mutilated
disabled disfigured dismembered

Origin:

1350–1400; ME maheym, maim < AF mahe
(i) m, mahaim < Gmc; akin to MHG meidem
gelding, ON meitha to injure. See maim

names that never went on the pillar
on the corner by the courthouse

on other stones we read: **MURDERED**
BY THE RCMP chiselled & removed &
later on a yellow thanksgiving weekend
painted yellow once again on the grave
stones Bienfait cemetery & went on
in minds the men who fell they tell
in dust & wind & cave ins
& littered the stories we told
casualties they said casual
ties to those who turned away

P. MARKUNAS	N. NARGAN	J. CRYSHKO
(AGE 28)	(AGE 28)	(AGE 29)

refused treatment at the hospital and
earth swallowed them like a blotter

there is no beauty here only
stories written in red ink
so some would believe /corrected

the sky restored to cyan
by the removal of red from white
when they were written off

and years later the banks
in the valley collapsing
mothers warning children against
all the cavities in time
all the incivilities

iii

and the cenotaph we stood
before was it ’52? the symmetry

this would be the miners
                    in ’32 except it was
’31 (Sept 29) Dieppe in ’42 (Aug 19) no
symmetry only a stone column & on or in
the dead who never came back are there
where we stood in rubber boots

the names in columns
long lines of names
you can stumble on

& the coroners report years later
    finally on the other corner
flanking the courthouse

at the trial many did not know
)the symmetry of it triangulated
cenotaph & coal car kitty corner on 4th
                                        they did not know what
                    in English they were saying

iv

from Bienfait a new monument an old
coal car raised from the earth
September 29th, 1981

must have been a bright morning
an Estevan day dedicated half
a century later to the miners
and at the rising of the sun
and the going down
when crows clap past
and birds still bravely singing fly
someone's breath getting
lost in horn or bugle or cornet
snagged on barb wire caught
on bullet & bayonet & billet doux
smothered in mustard & methane & cyanide

& of those who died that moment a veteran
who did not die in censure wrote **they are**
defiling British Institutions so sure of himself
said the work was well done surely
a fait accompli well accompanied
in bullets & bulletins
and now we lie

v

on the earth
passing through
latecomers leave
penknife sentiments
erase the sediments
erode the pigment

a side where Jesse James or someone
climbed among and over the soft
    skin hacked letters
        into the hide
alongside but not over
(the ochre of) bird and sun and deer

decades later boys in crevices
gouged where Agassiz had exploded
crouched in the shade and damp
saw men in moccasins walking
birds and deer shining with ochre
clambered over beached whales
shelves they stood on bleached
by wind blistered on sun
and giddy with fear
            /that thrill
that (almost) entering

vi

        beneath the markings of
territory the pissing on bushes
the kleenex & condoms & broken
bottles by now hardly able to find

        what for hundreds of years
spoke to bear called on coyote waited
for deer listened to sun warm
        the rocks lifted their faces to
            the sweat and splatter
the shit & shaking & flies splintered

bones faint glyphs you might be able
to make out from over here
or perhaps there
where
you stand
the birds still bravely singing fly

one stone
a weight or mass equal to 14 avoir
dupois pounds (about 6.
35 kilo grams) avez
vous du faim? du pain?
la femme? a gram
ma or pa & what
's a livre worth it was
formerly used in common

wealth countries too 8
stones make one hundred
wait in imperial me a
sure since the term is
so vague it is hard
to know whether we should
speak of kilo
grams (in mass) or new
tons (of weight or
force) in keeping
with what newton
said in equal &
opposite in equi

valence which was
in any case always
imprecise a stone
of beef in London was
the quantity of 8
pounds in Hertford
shire 12 pounds in Scot
land 16 pounds

in days of stone
in days of yore in days of ore
when a stone was not
a stone as tonishingly

enough a 20-stone man must have been rock
solid built like a brick shithouse
hit like a ton felt a little
bolder than your average

man that or a little more
adipose having de poids to spare
being so poised so well disposed
able to stand
on his own
whatever-numbered feet

again & again :
as in war they sought
refuge in tunnels
: Moore descends
man of stone
he reaches inside the stone
throat stone chest plays
his part in the mineral birth

uncovers canal figures wrapt in sleep
arms shoulders elbows skewed
scores of them in winding clothes
sepulchres they wait in as later
he shows miners cramped and
glowing in the shafts

sees :

gelid shapes
sluggish protoplasm from which
heads lift
larval or mummified

rows on rows laid out as
if they were in a mortuary
in no hurry
nowhere to go

lie as in Pompeii
burned to statues in
Hiroshima sprayed onto rock

“the sea of sleepers” he watches
he scans the gaseous winds
the galaxies of their bodies
the edges of their lives streaming

hundreds in stone
caverns shoved under
ground dream streets aflame
the mass of brick and stone
crushing those who squirt water
against their falling
the city flaring into
a charnel house

doom
boom doom
booomm

blooming of bombs & **dum dum**
shrapnel above
the shells from which and in which
they seek shelter

one of them
miraculously upright

knitting !

scarf? baby

bonnet?

sweater for a sister?

shroud?

the wavery shapes he finds inside
tubes move slowly through

stone ribs in which they draw
the air that must be stale
and stinking
he draws their
breath makes
or takes on their death

many have lost
their letters stand
chastened & shivering in their alto
gether stiffened or stained
old parchment
no dates no places no names
among the heather
illiterate now
unable to gather their thoughts
or send them
the here & there wiped out

whole mausoleums fallen in
abandoned mines in the Souris Valley

some parts in the yard loll
decapitated heads
tourists step warily around

except for the grave
Burns with his thoughts has kept
for another & yet
another beside it neat & marked
(if only the quick & the dead
could appreciate) makes one
wonder whether
through the damp earth he can
sense us /old A.S.
adamant
his invisible hand below &
over
a stone that presses on his head his thoughts
iron gratings some smith has made

poet keeping faith
with him who
no adam lies
beneath the stone

the need to roll the stone from the cave
he stumbled inside
stone-blind, stone-deaf

hard of hearing
what could he ever feel in his stony sleep
whatever the keepers
of ledgers say

and we all go on sloshing our lives
whether like those whose heads or hearts
were stricken
being dead can smell us
if we might count
in adams myth

a green slab on which are etched
insects and fish
hints of corn and grasses

28 definite symbols
some of them appearing
several times also

shapes no one can be sure of
unlike any known writing system

the signs arranged across the surface
in apparent patterns that look like syntax
peculiar to the Olmec language
the earliest known
language in the americas

from 900 BC a green
tablet which contains
what may be a dead end

smallest pebble around which the hard
-shelled excrete their nacre
salve their conscience
line their own houses
with porcellaneous protection

peddle it as pearl of great price
through which some times

streaks of glue hold the secretions

darken into well-kept secrets
answerable only to supply
& demand

where was it
they shot
him & why
not he used all
the wrong words

though not so the story
in America goes he was not
active as a Republican he was
a good man but they shot him
for good measure
shot him for good
killed him bam bam for what he said
or what they thought he said
for what one day he might say
killed him for the word

perhaps it was only just
for the pleasure
though it may have been bad
a mistake he was
getting bad
ly out of line

one night he is sitting at home
his mother there & they are
drinking a glass of wine it's been hot
it often is & they have some wine
when coolness begins to come
& out of the stones
the lizards crawl though it is too
dark it is too late for lizards
too cool you might think yet
lizards squirm out
into the chocolate night

wear their leather pouches
a slackness hangs from them
the dry men from Franco
crawl out of the rocks onto & on

the rocks they can smell
blood & they
want some
thing to break

open a bottle
rip open some skin
Lorca for his words will do
he will die for those
who are without sin
he whose blood would run
coral red

death a prodigality in him
spills his life over
flowing into their canteens
the cartoon stories they count on
raising dust where in striking
pirouette they fight
what in them not even
Lorca's blood can slake
the crusted lakes they slither

they are good men they are
important men have said so
& say so still
they believe in blood

consciousness but
have no conscience

this is how they renew
themselves their shows of
nape & cape & gown
they have every right

they grow like cactus
they spread like lava
where Lorca died
saving themselves
hoarding their lives
their needles & dust
their blood & swords

saving themselves
up for Franco

& for Jesus
jesus did they ever

we passed the cows
every day shining
80 eyes that showed
their stomachs
where to go

brown rocks
shining
in grass

Noah
(for John Lent)

i.

ships flounder
on the rocks cooley
himself the old Noah
It All sits Wed
nesday, Sept
ember 22, 2010
next day too

on the hinge of the world
a boat on top of the Rockies
in Banff in Sin and Ara

rat rubbing
his eyes and writing
poems in an ark he rocks
out the days and nights
where he has been

washed up barely
keeping his head
above water sees

he is doing only

what every other poet
in his place has done

cooley thinks the deck is stacked
against him yet
(dock too
now he has traveled
abroad he ministers to what
ever has crowded aboard

understands he should give up
casting aspersions

iinn the bluu-uuu Kuh-
Nay-Dee-uhn-Raw-Keys

ii.

inside a boat (it was
on the good ship Elsie K they call
it rescued from the Fraser and the Skeena
shaped like a bird's belly and fashioned
of cedar wood mahogany
that he puts to sea
that he has come to grief

cooley hunches very like a pig
realizes he should be better
of snout nimbler of tongue resembling
perhaps an aardvark in dark

knows his friends will groan his editor roll
heirs eyes and nays at this
                    his latest folly

          flatlander cooley
gawks into the mountainous cold
the unfathomable night

                    hunkers inside
his skin under the 2 by 4s
that overhead shed rain and snow
wonders out loud what words are out there
and whatever's a cubit and whether Louis
)Agassiz for
          one(was right

iii.

His hair was weedy, his beard was long,
And weedy and long was he,
And I heard this wight on the shore recite,
In a singular minor key:

iv.

snoops for halibut scans for salmon
supposes they must be out there
somewhere attending their own schools

when the light is thrown above & falls
     behind the walls he

sends out signals wonders
if he sounds like a submarine
at the bottom of the ocean
whose watery membrane
wraps the fish wonders
will he find a word
or code (LCK perhaps?

will one ever bounce back
bright ping on the brain

                    what will come of
the creatures in their stray and wander

v.
hour after hour cooley so
      recently shipped from
his dry-berry low-ankle prairies
squats in a thing of boards and nails

hasn't a clue hasn't a prayer yet
he waits with baited breath
      asks himself

vi.
he casts aspersions upon
an unbelieving world
casts his knotted thoughts
upon the waters trolls for a vision

waits with the foolish hope of the poet
endlessly drops his lines into
a bottomless world knows
he is not cut out for this

casts for a version of poem
he might pull out
something thrashing
                    on the end of his line
      with which to stock a stone
-boat some hoard on which he might
                   ride out the darkness

vii.
at last sends begrudging
and fog-throated raven
through a fudgy world to search for respite

something which might   sting and bite
which when the waters abate
he may take back with him into
the wicked and whirling world

which may or may not listen

hog line
no nonono
lady
you sweep me
sweep sweep sweep sweep
not: off
my feet well
that too but : to
the button it hits
the spot
every thing so right the angels weep
the sweeping beauties awakened
all 7 or 8 of them

that is why
however rocky things may be be
tween us we can always
hack it in the end
when i say that's it that's
the last straw & you say
let's call it a draw

& you know you
can always
take me
completely
for granite talk me into
your bonspiel
any old day or night
id go for your spiel
grenades going off under the heart

1700 pound black
slab broken on the corners
the front buffed smooth

from an ancient temple
where once it had been
part of a stele official decree
Ptolemy, 13, the Youth who has appeared
King in the place of his Father broken
some where some time
except for the careful scorings

three bands   three sets of writing
all of them worn and interrupted
the middle incised in "demotic" script
three languages that puzzled for years

readers learned 1400 years later to open
the 3rd band in administrative Greek
the Egyptian hieroglyphics locked on the top

1799 stone pulled
out of an old fort
exhumed from an ancient temple

centuries later
Napoleon's armies hauled it up
up it rose from the ruins at Rosetta
rock out of a frost boil you might think
or petrified gland

2 years later seized by the British
and installed in the British
Museum 1802 the chisellings
highlighted in white the stone
coated with a layer of carnauba
wax making it dark and shining
meant to protect it from
the soft touchings of visitors

in 1999 the "Cracking Codes" exhibit
          removed the deposits
printer's ink human smudges white paint
highlighted the lettering that emerged

for over 200 years stone
inside stone
in the British Museum

except for its burial
in the London Postal Tube
Railway at Holborn
safe from bombings
safe with Moore's
human windings

the latest of its gestations
2 years in a station 50
feet below ground until
brought back & lifted
into the streets

sits now inside a case
glistening in the light
where faces lean
press noses against
touch lightly with
nose lips fingertips
feel for a key
that may or may
not be there

and there was the guy
who showed up

a slab?   slabs?
two? three? more? under
his arm (arms?) did they
        scrape his forearms did he

weary on the way down stumble
did he heft onto his shoulders
        stop to clear
something from his eyes catch his
   balance catch
                his breath
where it tumbled down ahead of him

        sandals small respite from
scandal or bruise little protection where
his nails were broken and chipped

did he cramp?
    his chest tighten?

did he fear for his heart? feel faint &
unsteady in a sun that scraped his head?
did he want to wipe sweat
from his eyes that burned?

did he feel "duty done"?
a flare of anger he was
too old to climb or carry?

would it be probable he
dreaded the sniggers
set himself against averted faces?

he must have imagined neighbours
whose stone faces waited
among pools of dust & scabby rocks
saw in his head the sneers of neighbours
before he was back heard
a wife's scoldings &
winced when he saw her
children avoiding his eyes, their own
        friends all looking

did he wonder if anyone
            /if he himself
    could read the signs?
or would?

roche percée
dangles from the ear of god
a tear where it is pierced
six miles from where they shot

the miners & jesse
james once carved
they say his name

old lines odd shapes written
on the granular hide
and later punctured
an excitement of graffiti

bird voices under
a palimpsest of coal blasts
earth rumbling buffalo
the winds roaring
and the quiet of deer

the NWMP
their names & initials

TENN*EILLE*

BOB

MAC QUARRY

F.S.J.
LARSON
N.D.
1920

their incitements to death

shiver of flies
gather at the wounds
cut into the flanks
the face wearing away

the skin sun has tanned
people have riddled with paint & knife

only the strange & wonderful
porpoise holds
against the west
wind alone and pointed
as if on purpose
north in unmoving

unmarked by
what anyone might once
have said or ever written

the book that is scotland now snow
paqued whited out
a blizzard of plaque on teeth
& bones that may or may not be found
beneath the tablets

& Argyll having piqued the king
on a plaque in St. Giles has the stones
to stand up to the king & say
"I set the crown on
the king's head. He hastens
me to a better crown than his
own." dies on the small
and frightening machine you can
see in the museum. black and small. it does him in.
did them in. thousands. a plague on them, nothing
could placate. that and the gallows, they loved the
gallows, the old

order set in stone. how piquante
the fits it threw. how fitting
its tantrums, necrophilia.
it loved
to decapitate. replicate.
incapacitate.

they lost their heads
the whole lot of them
the king believed
or so conceived

they had grown
unruly & unduly conceited
and so a second time relieved them
of them.

snac is co-ordinating the old
fashioned move of a large
stone the st norbert buffalo
stone from the oak
grove a distinctive forest once
part of the trappist farming
enterprise now part of the south
wood golf and country club
lands as the stone has
deep historical and spiritual
importance to this site
it should be
moved where all people
can continue to visit

and enjoy it snac
has undertaken to create
ceremonial grounds where
the buffalo
stone may come to rest

would like to invite you to come and help
with the moving of the buffalo stone on july
12th 13th and 14th please arrive
at the snac building any time
between 9 am and 3 pm consider
participating for a 2-hour work
shift we will need extra hands and strong
backs with shovels ropes poles pulleys
and stone boat we will continue

the ancient tradition of many
peoples of the earth the ceremonial
moving of large stones

(for Eli Mandel)

i

a lighthouse the house of light burns a dark ladle churns your
brain rehearses wipes across speech a spoke a branch a blade
of light a crow calls out calls to the black glass the lamp the
cow spooked jumps over the spoke turns & turns you yearn
for something to wash up on night one night only you cannot
wake to the small stroke the tongue the slight tear the far room
your hands your fingers open for its weight in your hands cuts
till you wait on the ticks the clock swipes off your face the slow
garbage of night & silence

the world slaps up against the shore on your face laps laps laps
the brightness lashes against

ii

light sideswipes your body up & down a broken brain bobs
up and down the slope you float inside a clunk of oars water
splashes your face loses itself i am here i am here you want to
say ice on the sleeve your coat forms high in the rafters above
your brain a broken fan all the sounds jammed

iii

a small boat strokes toward the rocks rides on the light its
whisper i am here you say you try to say light light has become
sticky is stuck in your throat the locomotive its noisy eye when it
lasers your head wrecks on the coastal rocks the corks you catch
the coarse gravel breathes a splinter of light a jagged radiance
you row & row through the night the terrible roar of light

iv

his mother he said knocked
down by tiny strokes for
him for her the worst
was when they cut
out the tongue

v

the silence behind his eyes
the machine in his head
                            & no
    where
              for the
electric
       city to fall like snow

lines snapt
yanked loose
& no one to speak
no one to answer

the quick silver light
sharp sliver in his brain

what is it so say something
happened is happening
when we are touched & we come
into speech that we are
in an old story

it's an old story
¿ isn't it

the livestock somewhere gazing
a two or three
storied house   a deep cellar

the rocks i swear glisten
the very sticks listen
listen you say
your steps
keeping time

music travelling in silk from your throat
where you up and   ¡ shove off

breathing like a lighter
moving like a scarf in may
all the way home

the air in Scotland slumps
also humps
old geezer who coughs & snuffles
in glum intent bunches
until it

breaks & slides
off the sky
not in chunks as you might expect
because there are no edges there are no breaks
and it dumps cold

so there they'd be, the clouds,
punch-drunk they'd slouch around
in rheumy-eyed congestion
their stomachs would sing more
keenly than bagpipes

so tubercular you could hear them
breathing they would lie in soggy torpor
after days and nights of sucking
whisky out of the peat
they would be badly hung-over
their hair matted their feet
numb from slogging through all that porridge
they called weather

people in hiding, Coven
anters in disguise, meeting in
open fields covert they sit among
rocks & stones of the fields
sit or stand or kneel
converts to heresy
their acts of ecstasy
subject to gossip   hearsay   false witness

they are not lilies though they stand among
& are of the field the authorities would have
filed thru
black flies at carrion

so they would not be surprised. could not be
come upon. nor cornered.
strictness of their own uncom
promising
so they could reappear
bringing in
singing in
a better word
a matter of which craft would get them there

dyed-in-the-wool christians
lambs to the slaughter
dyed for the sake of the word
come unto me they heard someone
say coming through the rye
bringing in the sheaves

rocks in the new museum
itself a huge stone
with lots of time inside
lots of rocks too
& clocks that measure

Nazareth in a pub
across the cobbles singing
love is a burning stone

at the standing
stones on the Heb
rides, is it? the ones on the Scottish
islands, hills so low and so
sweeping they could be
the place where the world began (or
ended(amid

long wild grasses
sheep who sleep in their parkas
pay no heed to wind
swerve and rain drift
must for most
of the year slash through

the store near the standing
stones at attention

they must answer to a standing
order from god their jag
-toothed hunger no wind can feed
no more can
the standing sheep and
tourists in rockports

he carries away four
smooth agates one
dark blue with a
lighter centre
10 years later
he pulls
open the drawer
looking up at him
a blue eye

: the small stones
liquid with colour
fit finger & pocket

and this one
the brown stone
flat and round almost as the moon
in the palm
he polishes
with his nose rubbing colour
and pattern the way the
woman in the story did,

the pipe for, was it? her grandfather
the colour and pattern rising

They tried to explode one of the towers with dynamite **whhummpp** & barely budged it, a few inches at most. German workmanship. This in the tourist guide: "A short summary of the history of Heidelberg." Some guys put up castles, bring in galleries, sometimes galliards (the foppery), every one of them, enter into treaties, marriages, alliances, stack up stones, such drollery. Other guys question marriages, dispute alliances, barge in, blow up castles burn towns. First guys build castles bridges marriages alliances galleries. The other guys, bad guys, show up with dynamite & malice, blow things up. They carry on like that for centuries. Big quarrels over rock piles.

This is when lightning isn't doing it to them. Lightning knocks off quite a few battlements. Imagine the bafflement—God strikes where the French could not. Something there is that doesn't like a wall. It's got them stumped, the French. Friedrich and Konrad and the Kaiser and the Kurfürsts and the Electors Ludwig and Otto-Heinrich and another Friedrich and Karl Ludwig—folks like that, they keep talking the local folks into throwing up stones all over the place. Hey, isn't it about time you guys were getting after a few more stones? Shot-putters, the lot of them. A nation of stone-throwers and shot-putters. Wall comes down, kein Problem, folks toss up another one over night. All over Heidelberg walls are going up & coming down, stones stacking & falling till they develop a fear of heights, a lot of bruises, till you'd swear they've been reading some pretty odd poetry.

Lot of guys blow their stacks, start slacking off, they get new guys onto the rock piles. They shall not cease from mental strife, nor shall they rest—not until all is wall in the kingdom of stones.

the air gurgles & people glug &
ladle their way inside
a bowl of oatmeal they call earth

people wade through
scotland dreaming
somewhere there is
a hot & terrifying stone
that sears the sky
burns off the very heavens
& they wring their hands
sorely afraid

dread in their heart of hearts there is
in faraway places such a thing
a scalding rock
from which light swarms
hot & stinging

or so they have heard
and in part do believe

By night The Stone of Bologna gives off
colours it has stored by day
all day it has saved.
theirs is Daylight Saving Time.

It is a dense stone. Its phosphorous drags in light. Once it was thought to be the philosopher's stone that could transmute base material into gold. It could improve a surd and dirty world, lift it into a shining. That new.

It proved to be a Luciferous Stone which did not itself produce light. Self-absorbed, it took things in. It took in everybody. It stole light. It hoarded as much as it could. Took as much as it gave. Positively Luciferian carrying on like that, something awful in the night.

And yet the stone could never contain itself and it overflowed, ran with an excess of light. It leaked, leaks still, into the Italian night.

If you ever get to Bologna you could check it out.
You could look it up.

the Stone of Destiny
the Standing Stones
of Cavendish the Blarney
Stone the Stoneys (in Alberta)
Turnstone (in Manitoba)

would this then lead one to
Estonia (Catalonia) Stonewall Stony Brook Stony Plain
Stonehenge where the world hinges and comes unhinged stone
timepiece where time is singled from the seasons hence a
wrench in cosmic machinery a jerk much less

Grindstone Point Stone Haven Red Rock Roche Percée Rocky
Mountain House Stony Plain the Rocky Mountains Little
Rock Big Rock Candy Mountain Stony Mountain Gladstone
Maidstone Steinbach Milestone Tombstone Scotch on the
Rocks the Elgin Marbles the Pergamon Altar Nefertiti in
limestone & stucco the Cave of Altamira

found the words
rocky the stone stony
discovered to wind & rain
nests of them   in the dirt

where will it all end
up see what turns
up round & ruddy as turnips
grating and rumbly

the terns & gulls gorging themselves
    follow the plough
        listen for the scraping
            in one way scribing
                & then
    the other

in verses & reverses telling the same old story
        something to write the earth
every spring in line & scribble

                        the birds with high cries
                        shadow the fields
                        home home on the **O**

                        range the pages re:
                            are ranging when
                                under the passing
                         they darken

the man's hand over the earth
                    coming & going
            scratches strange letters
rubs breath of the seeds into the dirt
    in heat & weeds erased

a temple stone
small stone some thought slight
nothing to touch Herod's
five-ton quarried mammoths
though rough & unhewn surely
meant for the temple

there at a stone's throw
fling flang flung
sling slang slung

sing sang sung

brained him like an ox

on one gravestone
modern believer a new
sense of mattering:

near where Adam in his myth lies
lies also "Jacob's Graham" with his blithe words
sleeping in his old gray home

Scatter my ashes, strew them in air
Lord, since thou knowest where all these atoms are
I'm hopeful Thou'lt recover once my dust,
And confident Thou'lt raise me with the Just.

time on or not on
his side
nor all
the electrons in the uni
verse not though he should
climb with wit the twisting ladder of DNA
all the way to the first days roll
call it all up into
one sweet ball

Mary Anning
Lyme Regis   Dorset Coast
town of radical thinkers & parliamentarians
"this little vile fishing town defended
by a small dry ditch"
on the shore she   removes the broken shale
scratches & etches
scrapes   & shaves

a dental hygienist   cleaning plaque
time has deposited
bit by bit   grain by granule
her lessons read by what she takes
out of the chalky board
lessens the past and increases it
the ammonites rising into such
fine and intricate symmetry
only god could have lined

dissenting   poor   female   “provincial”
from a family of collectors
struck perhaps by her pastor’s words
the world created in a few days
October 23, 4004, said Bishop Ussher
and the need to study

piqued by curios scattered in the banks
snake stones and devil’s fingers
and discarded toenails and verteberries bezoar
stones gathered for health and prosperity

and magic underneath a sun
fuzzed to cold and blustery skies
she walks and wades the crashing
that sucks kids and barrels and tourists
to their deaths the tides she wears
          wear away   eons

          day after day after day
          brushes aside shale and
          limestone the winter land
          slides her dog crushed under

          month after decades wipes off
          millions of years beneath
          nests from whose plundering men
          fall out of the sun to
          their deaths on the wind

          loud in her ears she tears
          them out cleans & prepares
          teases them from the clay

the long & fluted ones
the thick ones and flat
the yards full of oblong and convex
her long coat whapping in the wind
a sky so heavy and stiff
words if she were to speak
would be torn & lost

awakens them from their beds
the dizzying cliffs she once held
under an elm exploded
the three women dead she alone
finds and brings back
her head crackling with electricity

the impeccable scaffolding
they once hung from
the snatchers of eggs
the Atlantic implacable & heaving
so far away did they hear only wind

(and gulls? the men on the cliffs
could they—Edgar? Gloucester?
hear the curlews mewling? could she?
a cliff whose high and bending head looks
fearfully on the deep

she jolted to life the dead
assembled she finds
the names of gentlemanly scholars

did she tremble when she
                    saw and reached
                  what few men or women
                  had known or could ever believe

would have touched with the exquisite
              pick of her devotion
ichthyosaurus in 1821 *plesiosaurus* in 1828 *pterosaurus*
another time also *pterodactyl* and in 1829 *Squaloraja*
would they have spoken in hiss & grunt & thunder

wondrous creatures never before seen
ladies and gentlemen the strangest monsters
as if (in flying) they had stopt /mid-flight
daring young men on their flying trapeze

Mary Anning her dedication so perfect
she sells seashells on the seashore
rescues with a lover's fealty
her feverish delicacy measuring the tides
that exposed would sweep her
under or wash them away
the enormous frames of the dead

stood where Arnold stood and heard
the grating roar of pebbles and the waves
surge in and draw back dragging and
      fling themselves

where a century later flying creatures
tangled in their high thin spinning
hit splat face first off the walls
      she presses herself close to

brittle insects   moths & mosquitoes
receding with her
into the long withdrawing roar

menhirs ("long stones") stood
at the top of the world, wind
in their hair, men and women pointed
their fingers at the stars. wondered
what lines they left in stone the flow of
molecules people
by their fires saw

in the sky they all were
going out at once up to their
ankles shins hips necks eyes
the black water putting them
out into the cold where it runs
& when it freezes smashes
like eggs on rocks.

Europe is a series of rockpiles
people live inside. Cave people
then, cave people still.

All over the prairies farmers
haul stones out of their fields,
comb them off like dandruff

the farms as you begin to enter the Interlake, just south of Gimli, on number 8, are strewn with rocks, millions of small white rocks, confetti fallen through to the bottom of Lake Agassiz, bird droppings, lizard scat

they build little cities on the edges
of their country. Does anyone ever
arrive hot and thirsty from far and
distant lands? Besides the snakes
and mice,
I mean.

hard **hard** you shout
i have never seen such ardour
such ardour i have never seen never
experienced adoration like this
on on on you shout
you have opened a door to my heart
gets ready
to rumble & it does they do
my rocks
yes yes yes
rumble
yes yes / harder
yeehhsssss
a low thunder i like
to think over the sheet headed for

where ever you have
tucked it over
the top
in the blue & red circle

i.

cranium they call the British
Museum the ganglia
perishable as ever crackle

shift shackles & chains & levers
& pulleys under the dumb
stone rite of coinings write becomings
a ramshackle world, the then almost
byzantine he said what was and yet
may come the rights of unprisonings
etch marks, etc., sketch inside the roof on its brain
as if once upon a scratch

ii.

stones within stone
still line the walls
the marbles missing
only here and there
bits from slabs across which
men cattle horses chariots
parade to their deaths
Keats saw or imagined

missing only what in being here
in the bronze pinnings
the leather reins
once held together
hand to neck neck to halter
led them unaltered
to the very end

when, he wrote,
we shall throw
off our chains & sing

small twigs & insects
set & glowing
inside the sticky gum

deep whiffs turning to amber
beads from poland
spit of coniferous washed
up from the black sea

now warm and
dangling from your neck

stones on her fingers
& belles on his bones

a stone as one would
have it as tone would lead one
stone to another and ever after

to atone
as stone
to set the tone
to be at one
with stone
alone with one

an other at the
corner of 1st &
main a stone
as tone goes
a stone's throw
a way as stone
as tonishes
as it tarnishes
sun varnishes
vanishes in dust
into thin air
precious & semi
precious stones

amber (and
if you insist) am
ethyst a thirst for
aventurine (also known
as goldstone)
bloodstone
carnelian
diamond
emerald

ruby sapphire moonstone aquamarine and somewhere
between garnet and iris jade and lapis lazuli and jasper onyx
and opal tiger's eyes and cat's eye sapphire and turquoise
Araucarian Pine Petrifed Wood

agate gathered from the shores of Boundary Dam, Long Creek
bottled there, a gate in the earth, cut and polished, abolished
pit and grit, rubbed till it dully shone, when wet shifted to
light, filled with colours

AGATE: A fine grained, fibrous variety of chalcedony with coloured bands or irregular clouding. Each individual agate forms by filling a cavity in a host rock, infiltrating, filling the interstices. Agate, being porous, is often dyed or stained.

in aggregate great
as moonstone
birthstone

touchstone sounding stone key stone wet stone whetstone
capstone rolling stone field stone river stone curling stone
grave stone stepping stone wellstone millstone (around the

neck or not, lifting an uncle at the mill) brimstone firestone
hearthstone heartstone rock of ages rock solid rock lettuce rock
salt rock on stoneware petrified wood which in Banff explodes
in reds and purples, swirls and clouds of, whole table tops cut
from trees turned to mineral and buffed like shoes

such a lapidary interest
dilapidated minerals
pileated woodpeckers
pleated syllables
incomplete processes
incomplete passes
also when in football
they give him the rock

peach stone cherry stone
gall stone hail stone kidney stone

crossed the open
world to
:

sand
stone & berry
stain came upon strange dabbings
fingers over scratch & icon
every thing open almost to rain & sun
& an iron wind
: saw them

saw then :

it was not the rock
per se
it would be a late & certain
person or persons who
parsimonious in gentling
in chisel & hammer
will pierce the skin carve their own
names upon & beneath
& above some species
pisces that slid
the gravelled souris
(since the 30s muddied)

then saw :

where the wind had chipped
sediments time dropt behind
hacked gullies rivened clefts and caves
rain had wedged
some of them into stoves air cooled in
till sun escaped

speared every thing spared little
or no one scoured
the face of the rock
peered through holes
it had drilled
snakes wintered

between what others marked once
on the surfaces & those who gouged
their ambitions made their pass
ions later known in stone
that had stood for eons ever
since ice slid & torrents of water

a sky now & then scripted
the whole horizon scribbled
with flying & tumbling
with thumping & trembling creatures
birds & bison their markings
barely discernible beneath what
has been and will be

roche percée :

a strange strangling then
a series of lost sounds
deep wounds in the valley

know :

signs southeast of what will be estevan
the sun will address us undress
itself hang on the line to dry
our various & sundry stories
bake our muddled thoughts
& winds will shake
lines we make
& cast

we will be brought no doubt to doubt
our days to times of drought to
sloughs dredged of frogs to rivers
dribbled away
filling with silt

sticks & stones
in some sun

blasted places where light
festers buried
women being of
the earth /earthly up
to their necks in & of it and so
wanting ballast not un
like a shoe
on a last
as is only fitting
as having been accused
stand accursed

others stand
on their honour
more or less
at a stone's throw
prepare to sling
reproach using well
chosen words big
enough to cause

considerable damage
but small
enough not to

work too quickly small
enough to make it
      last to have
a lasting effect teach
a good lesson they

deliver just enough
     what is just
ly deserved for
seeking wrongly for
not for saking
and for having
got some pretty
funny ideas in
their heads too big
for their britches for
some blessed reason for
  seeking some

thing more or
        other
than they right

  fully should
            & do not

in any way
in any case
(let's face it)
deserve

they have met their fate
feet-first a fait accompli

they got
what they deserved they had
to act
the 50 men with a truckload of stones
before 1,000 onlookers had
to batter Aisha to death

as it was
written
as it was said

they were good men
and they meant no harm
that was the last thing they wanted
the last thing on their minds

the old churchyard,
cemetery, Grey
-friars cold & damp
the ground slippery

yard a rabble of broken
& dissolving stone
time a lime whose solvent
solves nothing saves no one

May 27, 1661
– Feb 17, 1688

today—June 1, 2000
when we are there, this time
one of the times
and between then—just
beyond a quarter century—18
,000 hacked snapt strangled
til they were stone-dead
/dead dead dead

all within a stone's throw of the church
the stone hearts of certain
(or terrified) belief
terrestrial sorrow

Marquis of Argyle
(did he look
them in the eye /eye of an eagle
the 1st and the last
James Renwick 18,

000 beheaded hung beheaded hung
one after another after another after another
severed squeezed broken chopt
up & down high street dragged over

stones hauled out of small prisons
open to cold & wet
their wrongs in bearing witness

rows now closed off but there still
walls & iron bars
strung down one edge of the churchyard
they could have been exhibits in a circus

onto scaffold after scaffold
the cobblestones jammed with singing
the badly mauled bodies separated from
their heads their loves their families

psalms drowning out it is said
the roll of drums
under the r's of their faith
under the head stones they laid
their heads under

poet John Murray, Edinburgh College of Art,
a show (with a photo
grapher) at a small town,
fishing
/poems

Tom Brian dropping us out front
joy at finding
inside   the rain

the power of proper nouns
in the fonts darken
across the whiteness
the fonts grow & squeeze

the shape & motion
letters move   like fish

as god is your witness
strangely stir

their bare-rock naming
stories eddy around rocks
on the postcard you carry home
in your pocket a package of paper stones
ink swims like minnows

for a few minutes some days
when we've been here ten thousand years
bright shining as the sun

the sun angles through the locks and looks
almost spiffy its shoes shined it could be
a burnished angel
newly renovated but before long
scuffed again
laces entangled in weather
before noon mired in gruel
glued to the bottom of a bowl

things get pretty iffy by the time
moon in its serge & tweeds shinnies up and
so help me god
before our very eyes
becomes a haggis

hugs us in its beefy arms
holds its sides til
long past
dark long past its prime its marshy breath
day & night
in expectancy & perhaps grievance wheezes
its whistly talk skirls in our faces

prepared to do its worst
and it might
get the best of us
it is that keen
that gassy

might because of the clouds
get splotchy and hang around
until they can fill up
on oat cakes & scones start
feeling fibrous with virtue
scratchy with goodness

to be stoned
is to be

stunned by the righteous
shunned by the good to be
oh tobetobe dobe dopey two
sheets to the wind juiced pissed

intoxicated, alcoholized, blind, cockeyed, fried, light-headed, inebriated, inebrious, looped, muddled, pixilated, polluted, rum-dum, slewed, slopped, sloppy, soshed, sloshed, sozzled, squiffed, tanked, tight, unsober, wet, befuddled, bemused, besotted, dazed, dopey, fuddled, loopy, maudlin, sodden, soppy, sotted, tipsy, boozed, guzzled, imbibed, nipped, soaked, swigged, swilled, tanked up, fuddled, maudlin, merry, tight, well-oiled, soused, into the sauce, intemperate, boozed-up, feeling no pain, besotted, having a nip, swigged, tippled,

carousing, getting plastered, washing away one's woes, swilling
it down

is to be:

on a binge, a bender, a blowoff, a spree,
a tear, a toot, a blast, a hoot

is to be a(n):

drunkard, bibber, boozehound, boozer, fuddler, carouser,
imbiber, inebriate, inebriate of spirits, lush, rumdum, rummy,
soaker, sot, drunken sod, sponge, swillbowl, swiller, toper,
tosspot, tippler, a stiff, a sot, dipsomaniac, barfly, rummy,
drunkard, wino, juice-head, guzzler, imbiber, drainer, partaker

to be stoned (drunk)
and so to be thus to be stoned is to be

besotted three sails to the wind addled beery corked crocked
flustered groggy inflamed jugged loaded loopy mellow muddled
nipped pickled pie-eyed pissed as a newt polluted reeling rowdy
pissed to the gills passed out rummy sloshed pie-eyed smashed
stewed stinko swig-taken under the influence under the table
feeling no pain under the weather under the circumstances
zonked hammered stone drunk

completely stoned

feeling no pain

Trier. The Dome.

A giant's skull. cracking open. losing ground against the weight of the world. all that air, all that toing and froing. all that yelling and sighing, all that chewing and gulping, towing and shoving. all that. a frowning. a frau-ing.

a lung crushed. a cave-in. a splitting headache, unheard, in the cavity of bone. high up the wall a huge wasp nest music drones from.

stone vessel on its way up
or down the Mosel

somewhere between Trier & Koblenz
four enormous barrels carrying wine

the rowers with & without their faces
dip 22 oars into the water
and at the back a curly giant
"merry steersman"
and another one
so stoned his head
has blown off and another
on the other end facing
everything out of proportion
the ship itself a little tipsy

the floating of wine over water
wine inside a stone ship
a warship apparently
yes your worship it is
a flagrant worship of wine
afloat in the Rhenish Museum
in replica ploughing across
    the invisible waters
that flow through the streets of Trier

the ones she gathers at Willow Island, off Lake Winnipeg, st. ones. oblong. bending and picking, taking and discarding, back bent. selecting the granite. with the care of a jeweller. patience of a scholar. devotion of a nun. studies them. checks for fleck and speckle, fit in hand.

up to the ear, head tilted, listens. can she hear them ticking?

holds them to the candle of sun. does she see inside them red and gold suns that look like lava, move with the heft of honey, slowly?

find inside them the huge red spiders?

she looks for the blood spots, picks only those
whose specks speak eye and beak, heart and
membrane. a choosing. the chosen ones.

hauls so many the island fears it will
slide with a blup into the lake

small eggs she lays in our back yard. and waits.

later, tired from attending, losing faith, little red
riding hides them in baskets passes them on
to a friend who rides horses named slurpy and
baboose

they sit in pails lining the back of her garage,
faintly humming.

hard now to gauge their size and shape and
weight much less know under the press of cold
and snow when this winter or spring in loopy
necks and wet feathers they will peck their way
out, return to the sun, engorge its heat.

> one morning when she wakens she will
> wonder what to do with a yard suddenly
> full of chirps what to make of the feathered
> lizards clacking and scratching and no where
> to keep them and no way to explain and no
> where to go

What if you too had listened to your own inflammable thoughts, if you had hung your heart out, a shingle, advertising? What if you were to have slung it, that swollen and inflamed organ, small boulder, over your shoulder and made your way through high passes, climbed up and over the cold, chest crackling, your balance lost, against all that is close in you? Your sudden and gusting emotions. What if you skulked through the drizzle, slogged through snow-filled paths, ached to burn so brightly the sun sizzled out?

In your unseen heart—where you know is the greatest heat, the deepest hurt—you would feel it whump. You would feel a whack-whackk, the thrill of that. Imagine such a rush when you torch into life, when it is lit, your semi-precious heart. You would be riven by love, cracked open by wish, your old withholding crushed to powder by the high siren song.

Peebles, Ap 24, 2000

Bill Wood?

No, Bill Wu-ud.

He has lost six friends, pals I think he said. Would he say buddies? No, pals is what they call them—pals. Six of them. In the war.

You can see the plaques, he says, the weather has affected them, the ones from the second war. The ones inside there, they are all right.

Atlantic. North Atlantic. You name it, I've done it. They threw everything at us—planes, ships, torpedoes. I have seen it all.

A short man, glasses, hearing aid. Normandy. He was at Normandy.

They ask me why do you wear the medals? And I wear them for my pals who didn't come back.

A short man, glasses, hearing aid. Harris Tweed, blue felt hat.

Has dropped explosives into the cold Atlantic where subs lurked and cold stacked so deep there could be no fathoming. Another laying of charges.

Bill Wood. Peebles. The river full of rocks. His mind full of pebbles that slosh and grind in his thoughts.

Bill Wood is in the pictures we take away. He comes back with us. In the camera.

And the boys from Estevan dead
on the beach at Pourville sunburns
hung round their necks & the coarse
gravel they lie so stilly in—

the rest of the country too
where the sun slaps
all the faces
the streets and alleys lined with them
aligned & misaligned badly
twisted turns & sudden leaps the whoops & crooked
dives along boulevards inside court yards along

promenades toward steps small stones mostly black
or white in geo metric pat
terns men kneeling from
the heat have shaped and set two
-headed hammers with which they chip & fit

rectangular shapes and sometimes pointed
into insignia & forms of fish (huge round one
in Lagos) they lay their hearts into

          sidewalks day after day men bend
                                                  the sun pains
                        takingly select chip
          ping set ting they are tamping

          stones sink them into beds of soft sand devoutly
          pave the towns of Portugal
                                    that here and there
              sag or heave

          and when it rains shift
                    / shiny & slippery underfoot

IN MEMORY OF
CAPT THE RIGHT HONOURABLE
NEIL JAMES ARCHIBALD PRIMROSE
M.P. M.C.
WHO WAS BORN AT DALMENY
DEC 14, 1882
WAS KILLED IN ACTION NOV 15, 1917,
AT THE HILL OF GEZER
IN PALESTINE & LIES BURIED AT
RAMLEH

THIS TABLE IS ERECTED BY HIS PROUD
AND AFFLICTED FATHER. HIS LIFE
WAS LOVELY AND
PLEASANT AND HE DIED IN GLORY.
They go from strength to strength,
THEM IN ZION
APPEARETH BEFORE GOD.

the table
light & dark light & dark
: what the seasons ladle

tricks of the pen
shadows cut by sun

an old lady time blows by
tall at 92 as she could be
and small wells
worn in the stone
stairs where memory pools
sun a cyst
in her palm

her silver fingers
thimble thimble who's
got the nimble

fallen into a well
many went into (*hell*
oh hell **looh** a voice

calls as though through
a bottle (sits on
the table's welts

& on it a cup   its long shadow
& the broken corpse
a mosquito   in nylon thread

all summer
sun in bright spores drifts

shadows so soft
someone could touch

drink where they spill
the windows shining

gestorben—died
begraben—buried
the Müllers tell us

translate when we see the war
graves none who could
ever have warded off
time or gotten off
the long list of the dead

three acres of young men
gestorben begraben
would if they could
have grabbed for
what little to be had
in the last days ached
under the small rectangular stones

beneath the stark tufts
the coarse grass
row on row above the Saar
that down the sheer cliff
far below them flows

through Saarland my
grandmother's family home

dyed in the wool
they were dyed in the wool
catholics possibly & they died
in the woods

Bill Wood, likely
protestant, good
as his word
did it for his pals
he did
& they died
& some were damned
& all of them drowned
where the South Saskatchewan Regiment waded ashore
wadded with mud & blood

Porto cemetery. A cemetery off the street we walked up. Step inside. Long avenue laid with paving stone, little avenues & streets off it, or to it, small houses on them, white palaces, some of them, that light up the cemetery. Graves with windows with doors, doorknobs, locks.

A vacant town. Quiet. A town where the dead have gone to sleep it off? To sleep off death?

What if you knocked? Would they let you in?

Some are furnished with tables & pictures. Do they hold tea parties at night, slip into fancy duds and ask their friends over?

Break out the cards? Maybe when it's dark they slip in flimsy nightgowns out into the streets, curtains blowing gently, & in stealthy voices gossip about the neighbours, find lovers in whispered urgency, dance furtively into the night.

We are all one in death they say, and for a second we almost believe them. Where then are the graves of the meek and the poor? In some you can see the coffins stacked up, one to a cubicle, 3 or 4 high on each side of the street.

in scotland even the dead feel cold
stone cold it would seem stone dead
& resurrection men who would be warmed
we should have been warned are "grave tickers"

                    talk about gall they take
                    & leave ticks on the grave
with or without guilt their tricks of cunning & deceit
quick as sandpipers along the shore they

raise with their guile leave
no stone unturned overlook
no chance to stir up the dead

to make the stone
hard to draw
out the stoniness this is the first
thing a farm boy learns
to strike a telling
blow sparks for a fire say
or speed when you too
spin & fling
around & in your head
a small hard stone
which (stolen) yet may stun

your heart which could have been
should have become fat & soft
a dumpling in perorations warmer than
a perogie with love
in your fist from which it skipped
its flatness across waters that turn obsidian

it is this perhaps stirs the story in the pot
the poet's that is the poet's
spoon in the coffee cup
that hits the spot you said or should have
where we huddle up to the black-bellied stove

its theme: the lack of luck
a pain in the temple
a dream dumped overboard
in which thumping more
expansive than your heart
that is still
a stone /but larger

or smaller under the weight
of your waiting
your shoving off
fearing the pain or expense

when it could have been
a boulder in the pasture cows rub
loving its scratch its sheer roughness
crows stand & shit upon

in frozen rinks & hangars
you from your rumply wooliness
your ice-cold hands let go
all your fine sediments
squeeze them into

a flat-bottomed mineral
which grumbles over ice
thinking i may be a little
simple more than a bit slow

hoping to bump into
me where in open
-mouth shock
i watch
you snot-nosed & hoping
to lie
shot
rock wanting more
than any thing
in the end
to have & to hold
the hammer

last stone with which to
lay me low one blow

& that's it   I've had it
a brained & stone-dead mule

once you've nailed me
on the button

the word is out

the words are in
books: reading
them into
here and where

in black & white sequestered
something they call lithography

a scatter of stone
which when it clatters
/stops
inside the frames forms
something called writing

the streets of Lisbon quaint and thick
with poets who choose & chip
squint when they bend
to shape and discard

kneel with sweat
their necks
burn where they
knead & tamp
tap in black
among the white

keys you might be
tempted to call them

tesserae (highly ear
regular) the broken letters
their abrasions no man
no nor woman can
unfeelingly remove or will

the Standing
Stones keep vigil near Storno
way out on the Hebrides
in the raw Atlantic
have gotten together &
there they stand
/stowaways
jab their fingers
accusingly
into the winds

they are not amused
they are not impressed
not in the slightest

yes i wld
if ever there were

time enough or room
i wld lie

by you
always lady

i wld
lie till the last
crack of doom

& after noon
& ever after

i was dead & died
every after
noon & night

we wld lie   & sigh
in private places

when we were good
& dead

& the moon a rock
laid on our head

and why
honour the dead?
their thistled stories?
their silent whistles?

why do we place stones over
their bones
and write

Gone and Always Remembered
In Death and in Life
She was Loving / Loved

Here Lies ________

Beloved Wife Daughter Father Son
Child Husband Sister Brother Spouse
We Shall Keep Him Her Them In Our Hearts

and flowers?

people haul water
leave plants tend
small stones pictures of the dead
though not perhaps in scotland
)though yes says Dana *they do*

sometimes

out near the Pentland hills it was amazing to see little gardens filled with flowers and bric-a-brac. Many of them even had lanterns hung in the wee plots.

we tend to this
tend to do this
at stone houses tend them
small castles for our bodies

that never stir in their sleep
cast not even the smallest slur
a purple plum crushed
ledges upon which we put candles
photographs letters crosses bits of cloth
flowers grass poems sticks prayers pebbles
notes of intercession bottles medallions
to ease them in or out of sleep

ERECTED BY, we say. **IN HONOUR OF.**
HERE LIES, we read. **LEST WE FORGET.**
IN (LOVING) MEMORY OF. we think.
GONE BUT NOT FORGOTTEN.

They were here too, the people who set them, the stones, rose up in their magic of flesh. Were they shocked that they could move and talk, touch other flesh, feel panic flash and go out? Must have wanted to swim in it, enmeshed, speckle the dark waters. Knew what it was to be, quick, and chancing. And afraid.

Must have sensed bodies are flasks you drink from. That skin stretches over earth, a tattoo of stone, people's movings, to and fro. Over the face of the earth. Time closes.

Stones, they must have thought, someone must have, are the earth's bones, sloughed. What flesh was set on, tied to, pegged upon, hung from.

Minerals were earth's veins—what against the body's resistance, they wrote. The earth was one big body, it huffed and ambled, shuffled and bled. It belched and rolled, breached and heaved. In its wind was breathing and in rain something else. Small insects eating their way through the earth, scratching the skin, burrowing into mines. And they fell into the mind's depletion, chewed the veins out of the dark and the cold and when sun struck straightened.

Billions of explosions prowled in storms no one could see coming and went off bewilderingly inside. Told them stories of how the world moved in dark and disarray.

And do we believe   certainly once
did   that bodies do
not rest quite that we hear
on the ridges of the words our lives sit on
their low pigeon sounds
listen for their small exhalations, exultations
come upon us unawares & places
we must not step, do them injury, fearing
we might hurt

them under the ground
wary of edges hedging their chances
the long rectangles of their waiting
wrecked angles /angels falling from
their once-living
where they flailed

inside the earth sense the press
sure of our feet behind them

a gray film of birds swim through
the yellow heat they skim
their feet burning on the membrane
that sticks and turns very dark
and slick inside faces
inside buildings feel sick
when they hear

shoes on gravel
air that is close
faces floating up

what we need:
a wearing on the soul

the capacity to feel
a tiny stone in the shoe

            a measure of
the smallest unit of weight
the finest shiver of thread
that kind of scruple

the dolmens are tomb stones, rocks the dead dream under, laid for ever it must seem, loud in their rooms, or silent. dumb stones. the stone trees they sleep under, quick and dull men, puzzled or laughing women, hard pillows they rest their heads on nights that never end. the cloudy outlines of their thoughts.

the stones speak an ancient and gnomic language. given now to our unknowing to sententia and riddle.

the bare bones of our lives 5 or 6 thousand years before the wind scrapes off the graffiti, centuries swipe by.

what allowed people to string themselves across europe in a necklace of stones? marked time, marked place, packed the millennia into midden heaps? felt rain, through their hands saw sun in a warm red. must have wondered what under the moons when they melted would become of their children, if they would turn white with milk, their stones spilled, realigned by water.

& one that looks more like a long large phallus pokes into the
sky, the other one too, small hill on the edge of a farm Dawne
embraced.

near the cromlechs. farm of the almendres. the almendres
cromoleques. some gone missing, many still. doing their
best imitations of moons once they might have been calling
to. fat round things, pillsbury dough-boys, michelin-tire
men scratched with signs, their solemn comic-book speech,
watching from inside

two rough circles a gentle slope
silent congregation
among the olive trees.

farm house broken and shingles softened
from too much weather too much
yellow in the brick (red above
windows and doors) a few
cracks all the way

down to basement its field
stone rough and ugly to young eyes
floor in summer cool and fusty
a corner where potatoes lolled and

sometimes salamanders
from the dirt & stone &
thin pale arms of old potatoes
slid softly out

it is a stellar performance
                    up   from the cellar
damp earth & spoiled berries
                                        its softness
grown out of its skin out of the bin
                                                its must
      a damp meander

      acute reminder
this is long before fall
when the pumpkins turn fat
  & run wildly askew and
show off their belly buttons
hide their flat paler bums behind

this is when potatoes make their moves
lonely from months in the bin
drop their lepral arms around one another
                    fumble for love
      their pink eyes squinting

                                  : pale breath
  would come
                    its slow tail
turns with the light

    the wonder with which
we grow in the clean air
  greet it fallen in
a hole we have created
                into which we
    sprinkle sunshine

a chance we seldom miss
kneel when we shake loose upon it
shake with the love of gods
burn thousands of stars into its softness
help it turn to fire

one they believed
dwelt in and among them
as did farmers as did people
who went into
and lived there /inside
a peep-holed existence

a tone they felt & emitted
at once meant they were
singing those signing stones
were at one inasmuch as
stone would allow
the wind soughing & the sloughing of rain

at one time this would have happened
happens still

the time they went inside
insects within entrails
& some blew blue
against the insides
left the outline of a hand
clear as those
flashed by the bomb

thot
some
thing you   might warm
your mind
no clear
shape

worry stone

tumbling to
ward colour
a pattern

hard to know
the bumps and abrasions

took it
set it
for others
to see

& ad
mire

why do we write of the dead to the dead
ofthedeadofthedeadofthedead

the dead not dead then & we can speak
to them (must) speak
for they call & call
call on us call to us call us to them

stand bewildered we do not see or reply
though we recall them no one answers where
they unmoving sway
waiting to hear

when i write
of my dead mother the words
will do her no good or harm

yet i have written of her
of my father spoken with him & i
would wish
in some way i have
done this for the living

for giving perhaps
what excuses or relief it can
allow)once again(to stand
afraid to step or injure
)wince when we hear
their bird cries

on the lid of the world
sets of three crosses
low & rough-hewn
evenly across the space
sharp tufts of grass in the dirt
and small markers for each
maybe 8" x 12"

on each of them
: name
: date of birth
: date of death

the names of those who died
in the last days of the war
no more than kids many of them

come upon
suddenly shaken
all the graves so many graves
each one the same

the same small
stone lying on the ground
so many marked "unbekannter"
"unknown" Zirker says
this at Klausern at Zerich Castel
up the slope you have hardly noticed
and then the
sudden drop so far you
catch your balance

Dieppe, Pourville
upon the heavy gravel on the coast of france
their travels stopped when they stepped ashore
and lost   their footing
August 19, 1942,

May 26th, 2012,
hot sun
a patio

the two men are swallowing oysters
no pearls before swine
though the pebbles must chafe
whatever their conscience
or the memory of the small stones

the young men from a small hot town
lie forever face-down in the coarse gravel

the government asks you not to take
the small hot stones lodged in their bodies

Stony Mountain in Manitoba
it was here they put Big
Bear wrapped him in stone
sealed his spirit in
he whirled like Lucy
& felt or didn't feel

Roll'd round in earth's diurnal course,
With rocks, and stones, and trees.

on the other side the entrance
long narrow path you took not knowing
through grasses and wild flowers
apple trees in blossom
butter cups and held them

if she is yellow when you hold the flower
then she is your sweetheart & their laughter
their pleasure when they see & then
what is i think queen anne's lace & then

the graveyard around the church is hot
and we are pleased to find shade

franz asking what would you
call this place the graves beauty
fully tended as in augsburg
in 95 where dana in the churchyard filmed
                              the pile of eyeballs

an old man walks up &
                        when i tell him in pigeon
                      german i don't understand
   says they head to the Dom
      they go to find the grave
           the stone rolled back
                              He is risen.

a woman with a smile carrying a tall bronze
cross has with the others stopped
for coffee i am waiting
                                    for wolfgang
             we will fly in his plane

        over the mosel over the graves not yet filled
with bright flowers there in front
          many colours & kinds
3 women & a new one, new grave, i don't notice
until we are leaving its dirt heaped with flowers

the church itself small & cool
beige walls red stone arches 8 small
wooden benches the comfort of
sheer & simple shelter

& then around the corner along the side
(an old woman has set a few tables in the shade
& another, 30? and a small child
a third old and gawking at the pilgrims as they arrive
crust of bread dangling from her mouth &
down on the far side, past the church, suddenly,
                    —no warning

                                        there it is

                                                    /

                    you skip   expectantly
your kilt on the verge of coming
come pleatly undone you yourself
about to break into a schottishe

      line's good i say
when it leaves the hand
for the cold regions of space
              or your heart
whichever comes first

& you say **ON**
OHN AAAWWN

HARD you shout & i
bend over the broom
GO HARD   GOTTA GOHARD

urgency in the motion
laying down straw
HURRY HURRY HURRYHURRY
you have given me the word
& the word is full of ardour
the world is at our door

the ice where you wait has begun
WHOOOA WHOOAAHH
to melt with expectancy
who knows where this
end could end
up the end i mean
this could upend things radically

the noise in out-turns & in-turns
moving in their own trajectories
you cajoling coaxing as they leave
as they are arriving

the graves
filled with dead soldiers
many
18, 19
Nov, 1944
killed in the last days

Oct 18, 1944. The call up for the Volkssturm begins in Germany, with all able-bodied men from 16 to 60 to be conscripted.

on a stark cliff above the world going on below
near a sheer rock
wall into which men of god had
burrowed and dug as if for gold
strange miners lived their lives inside out
wore like ceintures the rock they had and had not
spooned out

they went from strength to strength
their lives were lovely & they died

And there also are Eli Mandel's sandstone rocks in Saskatchewan. He heard the unspeaking stones. Est au Vent, Alexandre Amprimoz said once. At least I do not come from Est au Vent, Cooley.

East of the wind, I come from east of the wind. Did Eli know that, standing with the western wind crashing around him, among the huge rocks in Spain, or France was it?, thinking of home, Estevan, the hot gritty wind, the soft stone pulverizing?

what do you cook it on
ein stein she says
ein stein
ja ja ja   ein stein
a stone you cook it
on a stone
a stone
yes you put the meat
on the stone and
you cook

you don't have to be an einstein
to figure this one she says

a braille that feet find feeling
their way which if they don't
watch their step when wet
they slip easily on
whatever style of shoe
or sandal they wear

dozens of men sweat and lay
down signs before an iron-fisted
sun they have taken
from small stores
small stacks beside them
shrinking day after day where they line
the streets of Lisbon

smack them down **thwackthwack** & press
    them upon us their
imprimatur the black & white musings

tourists when looking
  up walk over
uncertain what it is
    they feel
  in their feet

in lacquered stone or their own gray
  matter what it is
  to be among the purple
  trees they may be

  thinking or passing over
  a lot of people passing

  up the chance more
    than a few

  dogs pissing on the settings
  being neither in accord

  nor in tune with
  the dancing in the streets

you may think of nickel shining
but it wasn't that

spacious as the moon she said
just one wide stretch of moon wreck
and just as desolate as nothing
but black endless black and black and black
the rocks scorched
black as chimneys

you could feel the tarnish
coming out of them /the heat
they were almost alive

and there was a smooth bench
that looked like a couch we sat on
and the only tree around
one small spot for thought or romance

all night the whoosh & flaming
day and night month in and month out
the lava oozing
as if the ground were wounded

and later years later she
goes back /finds
a piece of rock that looks like toffee
smooth as hard candy

and just what X
actly did the theologian say
any way
to Ein stein
st. ein
I need to say
one could say
you may in play or plain jest
want to say

eins zwei drei
what's to vier
it's time for fünf
and yes to sechs

one stone two stone
three stones a scatter

it behooves us now to ask
what now & what
all that matters

so what
what's the matter

it's all a matter of ones
tone one stone at a time
the swinging of a
toms perhaps we
should leave no one
sun burned
no tone unearned
nor light turned off

not one ear untuned no tin
ear in a ten-year drought
it's just a matter of time
before we (all) get burned
by an era of doubt

said oh my mymymy not
so fast, my little mi(ni)ster
there is something
sinister in this talk of relativity
these flippant refusals of gravity
enough of the fearful
there's way too much
thought of incest & incense
the gravelly speech of stricken rocks
those words of me to you and on my word

he felt sorely afraid
the theolog that is
loath to get caught
out could not face the logic
afraid albert was trying
to pull a fast one

professor one stone
feared the very stars
were one spermatic spray
away from sputtering

out god's sudden cry of pro
creation damn right he said damn
right that hoo
ligan poet
listen to that
take that he says

who cares
it's all a matter of timing
he said
this talk of ligature and litigation

& he's back
at it
, kuli
in his denim and dennis zehn
hard at it
worse than ever
bad at
/space & time he says
they're the same thing darn near
if you ask me he
himself is terrible at seeing
the hole picture
relatively speaking that is

and no way finally
no way of telling me or
telling him much less
telling time
not though it arcs
on itself at warp speed

when things want to return
from whence they came the angels weep

that's when you got a pretty
warped view they said
to him in wonder the wonder
boy the one they called Ein stein
hurry up he said
it's time

that's what makes us

one said docked
or sad one said
stone brings us back
long before
we're gone
the way of
sand stone
way before
we've ever thought
or we're ever caught
heading out
on the last round-up

benchmark
(in memory of Birk Sproxton
1943–2007)

Thus, though we cannot make our sun
Stand still, yet we will make him run.

a sort of birthmark
"benchmark" you wrote

The term benchmark originates from the chiselled horizontal marks that surveyors made, into which an angle-iron could be placed to bracket ("bench") a levelling rod, thus ensuring that the levelling rod can be repositioned in exactly the same place in the future.

you who wrote also
birchbark birthmark
the marking of
word without
hyphen world
without "em-dash"

word without hesitation
without yet sit uation

a starting point
against which to measure
upon which we can be sure
as you assure me & every one
the word is found on rock
upon which we take stock

take soundings
learn to know our voices
how far out we are

the hes it
ation
the moment you sit
on the other
side of the bench
we way over
/here

you cannot see us
on the other side of the hy

phen a mong the ten
dig its then that measure
you & me as sure
as hand & foot numb
er out our days

in thumb & knuckle we can all
most see
the parabola of your life
wobbling up like a knuckle ball
a bouncing puck

all the in be
tween was
we are

in the en we are
a small dash – quick

dash to the blue
line – in side numbers
losing our breath

coming & going
the lives we spend ex
-tend
to the very edge

-of the line
-the end of
the long da
sh—

slug shrugs
darkness the cold
tile it makes a long
vapour trail until
it has left
all fluid in
morning surprises
what it has written there
parachute that failed to open
its length slung behind
death spilled on the floor
this you could say
do say is an anomaly

lines are what people put on
pages white as bone as smooth
muddy trails once
more they write
nothing more

people are porcelain
bones you say have
grown old and half
crazed with time

i guess you could
say that
time X-
rays our lives sun
ravages an A
-bomb alpha to O
mega prints
our ages in rock

we should up &
rise into our bodies
where they are
)no kidding
kicking their heels at the edge

drink the dark waters that have turned
yeasty with time
sudden and violent in storm

his lady gives him
the eye tries to
give him the slip

his lady sees him
seizes him
up
& stares him
/down

& he turns
dumb as stone

& he leaves
oh he leaves

her
alone

& what of the boy who slung aspersions
swung his tongue loudly round
his mouth grew
secretions pearls that passeth
all accretion marbles
that exceedeth stone

flung one small & cream-pearl insult
sent to bruise
enough to rebuke

drove it straight into a temple
where worshipped a wild & mighty devil
who later under a slightly larger one perhaps
would finally go there & so
lieth he

sticks & stones will break his bones
& so endeth our lesson our lanky and
slingshot speech
all the knuckles of not knowing

if they were in scotland
she might have
said listen
listen to this

sun & moon business
all this big dipper business

where do you get this stuff
off on this stuff
i have had more than enuff of
these stars you've been mooning about

ones you drag around on a sleigh
morning noon and night
and say
they are shaking

actually shaking the sky itself
how do you think it looks

when you stand there gawking
and the moon dings by
head high over the cold slate
hooves & wheels rattling
& it hiccoughs on its way
a runaway
ice-cream cart

don't know
what to make
of them nor of their
unsudden & sullen disposition
their propensity to big-belly it at every turn
belies all sense their thick bellicosity
can't figure what it is they have bargained

for they are nothing
like what on the prairies rumble
neither jagged nor ragged nor cumulus they are

badly sat
urated saturday sunday sun sat there
all day & all week too
knows what is it to be so
situated so unsatiated

so thick & fat-headed
so ponderous they must be arthritic
& they snuffle non-stop will never shut up

could well be curmudgeons & highly contagious
swollen to afflatus that will not end
when they roll in on a big lazy fart
and hug their sides

at times they turn abrasive
gangs of kids
gangly & scabbed

when the haar is twisted
tighter than Harris tweed & barges
in off the firth

it would seem growing
dour with the damp

old or young it is bad
tempered you might say a scorpion
a renegade preacher
who will not renege on his
ways nor forgo an antic rage

once we got a feel
for it i mean
if you don’t go
& get cold feet we could

bed down together
)) curling
((our toes
between the sheets
here at the Scots Tour
nament of Hearts
lamentations & gnashings to spare

the line i mean
i mean do you like my line
in no time at all
you calling line & weight
calling them in to a place
in rings & tangents
hauling the frozen planets in
from interplanetary motion
we would be lying
two we two could be one
up and heading home

more weight more weight
he said what
were they
waiting for
and they
plied him with words piled
still more upon
rock of ages cleft for me
he being stripped
naked back to
the ground board
covering him and the stones
set upon chest and stomach
one by one six men lifting
heavy stones setting them

that he hath no sustenance, save only on the first day, three morsels of the worst bread, and the second day three droughts of standing water, that should be alternately his daily diet till he died, or, till he answered.

from time to time Sheriff George Corwin added
his weight on top of the stones enjoined
Giles Corey to enter a plea
they had pressing concerns
charges to press the men
who were slowly squashing him to death

looked into his bulging eye shoved in
with his cane the tongue which had
been forced by the pressure out of his mouth

was aided in attendance by
Captain Gardner who had been a friend
or at least neighbour to Corey for two days
watched as the men piled on rocks

more weight he said more
in need than fear and
crushed to death still unspeaking
charged with witchcraft
his estate safe from seizure

take eat the minister said
later at the service as
always he had
take   drink this   do this
in remembrance of me

that is why
when you
find me
between a rock & a hard place
when you take me
in)i got to hand it to you
you should have
good draw weight
you should have it
down pat
in the end
you
could be
hogging
all the attention

π

walk where skin shines or could have
shone found shrines to knees
the simple love of feet

bits of bone in reticules carried away
a fever against all that is

could have kept time
held water in a stone

π

might have moved in a skirmish of now
a swirl in snow and sun
might have entered a skirl skirts caught on
faces fresh with cold
and warm bellies
full as jelly-beans

π

city a place full of zapateria earle
and no less earnest for that
it is for a poet to write these things
that might keep
up with feet
headed this way on
crushed bones bruised heels torn
nails toes that bleed blistered skin
sprained ankles in Spain

π

why not
their wish for
some thing
on which to walk
to hear the small
stomached bagpipes talk
in fancy shoes and socks and kilt
keeping time

π

something foot-loose and fancy-free
if only to be saboteurs
throwing shoes into the works

π

their 70 years
thankful for some
thing more than no
thing at all

and still they come
3,300,000 steps
to find a crypt
in which there is
or is not any
thing at all

in Blasius Garten the sour german cider
vietz they call it and it is no
mean fete to drink

cheers we say & raise
steins where the sun falls
light & shadow
among the trees
among our friends

the bugs kept out & the cold kept in
because we put a lid on things

not one of us stoned
/not yet

shell game

they douse themselves with night
through which they
flare in dark flames

they are lit matches
and they move in staccato
insects seeking sun
fizz in the 6 feet of water
that falls each year

they are pulling off
one by one
the handles on their lives
candelabra of the years they have
dropt & broken

who when you say gracias say nada
it's nothing don't mention it
could tell you what
it is

3 footsteps per metre
3,000 footsteps in a kilometre
1,100 kilometres to Santiago
Santiago de Compostela
which is James' Town
3,300,000 steps more
or less to the crypt
three million three hundred
thousand steps on the way

for 1,000 years pilgrims arrived
100,000 each year come now
scallop shells in hand
but not underfoot

where he has arrived
on a stone boat
lies now in a bronze casket

candles that light
for you
click when you drop
a coin
for them

the young man inside has turned to stone
a granite skull hung from his belt

he was supposed
to have given the moors one hell
of a shellacking and he

lopped off heads threw
interlopers for a loop
though he himself is now well composed

in spain slugs move as elsewhere
through the damage of moonlight
crash and burst
in a shine

here too spanish
onions come undone
the layers of their lives beginning
to peel the ions freed
in mad excitement

gourds break open almost
as easily as kiln-dried hearts
though peregrinos bearing shells
carry them to lift their thirst
faster than turtles on their way to
~~water rivers~~ somewhere

ours a grim age they say we tourists
emerge as pilgrims on a badly written page
our compositions lacking in conviction

the city in which lies a headless corpse
that might keep
up or company with
offer comfort to the bent

those who have learnt

to stand aloof and
from the rooftops of
their lives shout
their need
for shoes their wish for
some thing
on which to walk
their 70 years
thankful for some
thing more than no
thing at all

as luck would have it
in the same streets young men and women
in bagpipe and mantle dance they
are game they for one have prepared
their faces

to be silly already are ready & willing
every last one of them refuses to skedaddle
they all want to shilly-shally in the streets
on the shells the women too are rejoicing
move like veins
like fuses
hissing in foam
from the sea

gotta go hard gotta go
hard
real
haaarrd

our fair share of ends
if only you
hurryhard hurry hard
would whisk me
draw me
all the way all the wwaayy
in to the house **hurryinhurryin** ears ringing
we could do a little
house-keeping
so they will not catch something
and orbit heavily past

you know you can count
on that /the key ping that
i know we can
score big
if only we
put our selves to it

hell we could put up
an 8-ender /no question
that would fit us to a T

Thanks to Jamis Paulson, Sharon Caseburg and the folks at Turnstone for their care and expertise, and to Nicole Markotić who has read the text with an eye for mishap and a joy for what might happen.